FELLOWSHIP of PRAYER

2015 LENTEN SEASON

by Traci Smith

FELLOWSHIP *of* PRAYER

LENTEN DEVOTIONAL 2015

by Traci Smith

CHALICE PRESS

ST. LOUIS, MISSOURI

An imprint of Christian Board of Publication

Cover art: © Shutterstock

Cover and interior design: Hui-Chu Wang

Print: 9780827210981 • EPUB: 9780827210998
EPDF Read Only: 9780827211001 • EPDF Printable: 9780827211018

www.chalicepress.com

About the Author

Traci Smith has a Master of Divinity degree from Princeton Theological Seminary and is pastor of Northwood Presbyterian Church in San Antonio, Texas, where she lives with her husband and two sons. She is the author of *Seamless Faith: Simple Practices for Daily Family Life* (2014).

Dear Reader,

One book on my shelf with very special meaning to me is a collection of art journals published in 1997 called *The Journey is the Destination.* Photojournalist, artist, and activist Dan Eldon created the journals. His short life of 23 years was full of adventure. He traveled to 46 countries photographing world events, filmmaking, and going on safari. The journals contain incredible photos, social commentary, and cartoons. They were published after Eldon was stoned to death in Mogadishu, Somalia, while photographing a bombing.

I love Dan Eldon's journals for many reasons. They are vivid, personal glimpses of what he saw on his many adventures. Some of the pages show him trying to make sense of that which cannot be understood: war, famine, and injustice. Other pages are bright and cheerful: photographs of the people closest to him.

The title of the book, *The Journey is the Destination,* is also very meaningful to me. So often life is described as a journey, as it's a very relatable metaphor. Life has twists and turns, forks in the road, hills and valleys. Yet the metaphor of life as a journey seems to imply that there is always a starting point and an ending point, and that part has never resonated with me. The idea that the journey itself is the destination is a beautiful way to go through life.

This Lenten devotional is made up of what my preaching professor in seminary liked to call "slices of life." They are snapshots of moments in time that shaped me in some way or gave me new insight about God.

I hope you find some of the moments I have captured will inspire you to reflect on the moments in your life that have had similar meaning. Perhaps you will want to journal your own reflections during your Lenten journey. I invite you to share your thoughts and insights if you are so inclined. You can get in touch via www.traci-smith.com.

As you travel through Lent this year, I hope you will not put pressure on yourself to "arrive" at any particular destination. The journey itself is the destination.

Grace and Peace to you,

Rev. Traci Smith

ASH WEDNESDAY • FEB 18

You Are (Star) Dust

Read Psalm 8.

You have set your glory above the heavens (v. 1b)

"From dust you have come, and to dust you shall return."

These words echo in church sanctuaries all around the world this day as ministers and priests apply ash to the foreheads of repentant parishioners. The words are meant to remind us that God breathed humanity into being by blowing into the dust of the earth. When we die and return to God, our bodies will, once again, be the dust of the earth. On Ash Wednesday we take time to humble ourselves and remember that we are small compared to the great God who made the heavens and the earth. Here is another way of looking at it: instead of seeing ourselves as the dust of the earth, we can think of ourselves as the dust of the stars.

Every atom in our body is made up of the same matter and chemicals that the stars are made of, the chemical fingerprints of God. When the earth came into being, the matter of the universe became water and trees and volcanic rock and us. We are, quite literally, made of stardust. When we look at it that way, we're not small. We are big. We are eternal.

A healthy view of who we are, therefore, will take both extremes into account. When we remember that we are dust, we remember that our time on earth is finite and limited and that we come from our Creator and return to our Creator. We also remember that our existence is miraculous and that the "stuff we're made of" is the stuff of stars. Let us journey through Lent holding these two extremes together. From dust you have come, and to dust you shall return.

Creator God, thank you for making me from dust: dust of the earth, dust of the stars. Let me live my life knowing that I am both. Amen.

Thrown into the Desert

Read Mark 1:9–15.

And the Spirit immediately drove him out into the wilderness. (v. 12)

Two things happen in this passage in quick succession. First, Jesus is baptized. The heavens open up, the spirit comes down upon Jesus like a dove, and the voice of God comes down saying, "This is my son." But oh, how quickly the scene changes. A few verses later Jesus finds himself in the desert where he is tempted and tested by Satan. Not only this, the Greek word used for Jesus' being sent to the desert is a strong one. Jesus is not casually led to the desert; he's compelled there. He's thrown there, with force. I heard someone say once that it's almost as if the dove that came down from heaven transformed into an eagle whose talons reached down and grabbed Jesus, picked him up, and carried him into the desert, where he was dropped for his forty days of trial.

It's a hard but ever-present truth that we live our lives in the delicate balance between these two places. One moment God is commissioning us for greatness. The heavens open up, and God's voice is right there with us. Before we can get too comfortable there, however, we find ourselves expelled into the desert.

This Lenten journey will be a journey of both desert wanderings and baptismal promises. The best thing we can do on the way is to be open to the spirit of God in all circumstances that seem to be neither mountaintop nor valley, and to recognize that God will be with us in all of these places.

God of grace and love, draw near to me on this Lenten journey. Help me to see you in the ups and downs, the rivers and the deserts. Amen.

The Gift of Tears

Read John 11:28–35.

Jesus wept. (v. 35, NIV)

The other day I was asked to come to the bedside of one of my older congregants, who was in her last days of life. I've done this many times to offer prayers, anoint with oil, and provide presence and comfort. The space between this life and the life to come is a sacred space. I've been trained to have a healthy level of separation in these moments, to provide what psychologists call a "non-anxious presence."

A person who is a non-anxious presence is able to separate himself or herself from the immediate situation in order to provide comfort and calm. In all the times I've been at the bedside of someone in my congregation who was dying, I've never cried. I surprised myself on this particular day, then, when upon seeing Gemma,* I started to cry.

Maybe it was because she was all alone, and there were no other family members I had to be strong for. Maybe it was because all of the other times I visited Gemma, she was sitting upright with her pearls and tea and freshly permed hair. I was shocked to see her lying down, breathless, with matted hair and a sweaty gown. Maybe it was because I didn't even know she was sick, and the urgent call that she was dying came as I was on my way to go make homemade play dough with my two-year-old son. I don't know the reason, but I do know that it felt good to let my tears flow.

The tears felt cleansing and healing, and so I let them go, quietly. As I reflected on it later, I was reminded of the many theologians who have written about tears as a type of baptism, a means of grace. Instead of being embarrassed that I had somehow failed in an attempt to be a good minister, I started to wonder if the tears were given to me that day as a ministry unto themselves.

Lord, give me wisdom, I pray, to know when to fight back the tears and when to let them flow freely. May I accept the gift of tears to cleanse me and heal me. Amen.

Name changed in respect for parishioner's privacy.

The Wildfire Burns

Read 1 Peter 1:6-8.

So that the genuineness of your faith—being more precious than gold that, though perishable, is tested by fire—may be found to result in praise and glory and honor when Jesus Christ is revealed. (v. 7)

I grew up in Illinois, a state known as "The Prairie State," and I became fascinated with prairies in high school and college. When many people think of a prairie, they imagine boring green grass, but the prairie ecosystem is much more than one type of grass.

Prairies are just as complex and interdependent as rain forests. There's a lot going on in a prairie system, much of it underground and microscopic. Prairies exist in places too wet to be desert and too dry to be healthy forest. They are remarkable.

Fire is crucial to a healthy prairie ecosystem for two reasons: first, it burns away any wooded plant likely to choke out the many prairie grasses, and second, it speeds up the rate of decomposition. In other words, prairie fires are important because they remove that which is harmful and pave the way for that which is good. In my hometown of Batavia, Illinois, there is a large prairie restoration project at Fermilab, a national physics laboratory. Fermilab is less than a mile from my house, and I remember the controlled burns that swept through those grasses and the smoke that rose and filled the air.

In our lives there are often invaders that don't belong and new growth that must spring up. Though we don't relish or look forward to the fires, they keep us healthy. The decomposition of the old grass is what provides the fertile soil for the new.

God of new life, help me to see how the fires in my life are necessary to burn away that which doesn't belong and provide soil for new growth. Amen.

Changing Direction

Read Psalm 1.

For the LORD watches over the way of the righteous. (v. 6a)

My husband Elias is from Colombia and knew very little English when we were first married. About a week or so into our new marriage, we had one of our first major disagreements. I was quite upset and started a long speech in Spanish detailing my unhappiness. About two thirds of the way into my argument, Elias interrupted me and said—in English—"Traci, you need to calm down and take a deep smell!"

Of course, what he meant to say was that I needed to calm down and take a deep breath, but the word he had in his mind for "breath" came out as "smell." Take a deep smell. I got the point.

In fact, not only did I understand what he was trying to communicate, Elias's mistake turned out to be just what we needed in that situation. I thought it was funny and endearing, and I burst out laughing. It was a moment of levity in a tough situation, and I forgot what I was going to say after that. We ended up tabling the discussion and moving on.

As we journey through life, we often find that we need something to shake us up and turn us around. Whether it's a kind word, a "deep smell," or a change of pace, we don't have to continue in the direction we're going. We can turn around and take a new path, find a new way.

God of the journey, help me when I take myself too seriously. Help me to turn around and go a different direction. Amen.

Extra-ordinary Moments

Read 1 Peter 4:8–9.

Be hospitable to one another. (v. 9a)

The very first funeral I ever officiated was for a woman with at least fifteen grandchildren. On the day of the funeral, during the short reception afterward, the grandchildren sat around singing the praises of their grandma, sharing stories of her faithfulness, and laughing about their many happy memories. Except for one teenage boy.

This young man sat quietly in the back, staring at the wall, his face blank and expressionless, his knee bouncing up and down. I sat next to him in silence for a while before I finally said, "I'm sorry about your grandma." His lip quivered, and then the tears fell. "There was never anyone like her," he said. "She made her own syrup. Did you ever know anybody who could do that?" I answered honestly that no, I never had, to which he replied simply, "It was really great."

It occurs to me that the life we are building while we are here on earth, the life that we will leave behind when we depart from this planet, is a life built on small moments like these. We think that it's about the big days, the weddings and the baptisms and the graduations, but it's not. Those celebratory days are important and memorable, to be sure, but it is the pancake-syrup moments that add up to an extraordinary life.

God of the small moments, help me to see you in the ordinary, to know that each ordinary day is an opportunity to create something extraordinary.

Clouds and Fire

Read Exodus 13:20–22.

Neither the pillar of cloud by day nor the pillar of fire by night left its place in front of the people. (v. 22)

Wouldn't it be nice to know which way to go all the time? Today's passage from Exodus illustrates this kind of guidance: God sent a cloud each day and a pillar of fire each night to show the Israelites where they needed to go. Though the signs were clear, the Israelites still had to put great faith in the system that God had set up for them. To get to their destination, they needed to trust that the clouds and the fire would not lead them astray.

It occurs to me that GPS systems, computerized maps, and a variety of other technological tools are in many ways, modern-day pillars of fire and clouds. They lead us exactly to where we need to go, and they require us to put our faith in them that they won't lead us astray.

The real challenge comes, though, when our destination is not a physical one but a spiritual one. What if we need to take a journey through grief or out of a relationship? What if we need to travel through an illness or a career change? These destinations aren't found on maps. There is no GPS system equipped to show us where to go and what turns to take.

For these metaphorical journeys we have to look for the cloud and the fire in unexpected places: the voice of a trusted advisor who speaks God's truth to us, the Scriptures, the intuition God gave us, the still small voice of the spirit. Though these things are not as obvious as the fire and the cloud, they are just as trustworthy, and when we put our trust in God, we can be sure that God will lead us where we need to go.

God of clouds and fire, thank you for the signs that show me the way to go. Help me to trust that they will get me to my destination, even if I can't see it. Amen.

Knowing Scripture

Read 2 Timothy 3:14–16.

All scripture is inspired by God and is useful for teaching, for reproof, for correction, and for training in righteousness. (v. 16)

Obviously, I can't speak for all ministers, but I do know that sometimes it's easy to be surrounded by Scripture yet feel like it's somehow not doing its work for us ministers, specifically. In all the work of sermon and Bible study preparation, we've got our favorite translation open and the study materials all fired up. We're conjugating the Greek and Hebrew and looking into the historical context. Unfortunately, that's simply not the same as having the Holy Scriptures settling deep down into our souls.

I remember feeling the difference between those two concepts in a very real way once, in the wee hours of the morning. I was preparing for either a sermon or a Bible study or a devotional, and I was very tired. All I wanted to do was go to bed. As I flipped through the Bible trying to complete my work, my eyes caught these words that were underlined in my Bible: "When I fall, I shall rise; when I sit in darkness, the LORD will be a light to me" (Micah 7:8). In that moment, in my exhaustion, I felt that the word of God was sinking deep into my spirit and my soul. In seeing those words and letting them minister to my tired spirit, I felt the power and presence of the Holy Spirit with me.

If we feel inadequate when it comes to Bible study or knowing Scripture, let us always remember that knowing about the Bible and feeling the presence of God are two very different things.

God of the Bible, help me always to have an open and receptive heart, that I might hear what you have to say to me through the words on the page. Amen.

Pappy

Read John 10:27–30.

"My sheep hear my voice. I know them, and they follow me." (v. 27)

Lisa, a woman in my congregation recently lost her father, James. James wasn't known to most as "James," though. He was "Pappy." At the memorial service Lisa told a story:

"Before Pappy was Pappy, when he was just 'Dad,' he noticed that when a child shouted 'Dad!' in the grocery store, a great many men would turn around. This was unsettling to him. He wanted to be able to turn around immediately and attend to the voice of his own child anytime, anywhere, and so he decided he wouldn't be 'Dad'; he would be 'Pappy.' Anytime, anywhere, Pappy could come running to his children and attend to their needs."

Lisa went on to say that Pappy did exactly what he set out to do with his choice of unusual names. As "Pappy," he heard his children when they called, and he ran to them, no second-guessing, no hesitation.

What a beautiful example of God's great love for us. God hears us when we call. Whether we name God "Abba" or "Spirit" or "Mother" or "Holy One," God distinguishes our voice from the many others calling out and focuses on our unique voice.

Sometimes we are out of practice when it comes to saying God's name out loud and asking God to draw near. People say to me all the time, "I think God's got more important things to do than think about my little problems." I disagree, and I believe Pappy would too.

God of many names, hear us when we call. Help us to draw near to you, as you draw near to us. Amen.

Tangled Up

Read Matthew 24—26.

"My Father, if it is possible, let this cup pass from me; yet not what I want but what you want." (26:39b)

The necklace I wanted from my jewelry box was the thinnest one, and it was the most tangled. Many disorganized necklace-keepers like me can relate to the phenomenon of the necklace tangle. Of course, what always happens is the one you want is inextricably right in the middle of one giant tangled mess.

The necklace knot is a curious thing. The more you pull on it, the tighter it becomes. As I sat on my bed trying to release the necklace from its stubborn jumble, I realized how much life is like that. The harder we pull, the more entangled we become. To break free, we can't just grab a problem and start yanking; we actually have to dive into the middle of the whole mess and try and take it apart thread by thread.

This was the case for me with the necklace, and it's one of the overarching metaphors of the Christian journey: when we take up our crosses to follow Christ, we often find that our lives become harder, not easier. Sometimes it's simpler just to cheat our way to the top, to live lives of luxury while ignoring the suffering around us, or to eat junk food rather than a healthy diet. Just because something is easier doesn't mean it leads to wholeness and salvation. Let's stop tugging at the tangle and realize that to find true freedom, we need to confront the difficulty and start taking it apart, strand by strand.

God of the cross, give me patience and endurance when your way is difficult. Help me to see the big picture when the details become overwhelming. Amen.

Today

Read Psalm 118:20–25.

This is the day that the LORD has made;
let us rejoice and be glad in it. (v. 24)

As a pastor, I'm keenly aware that folks don't usually remember my sermons a year after I preach them, or even a week after. A colleague once explained it this way: Do you remember what you had for breakfast a week ago? No, but you do know that it sustained you and filled up your hungry belly. So it is with preaching. As with food, there are a handful of "meals" that you remember years later because they were just that special.

I remember a very special sermon; it was one of those that comes around only once in a decade or so. It was about this verse: "This is the day the LORD has made; we will rejoice and be glad in it" (v. 24, NKJV). The preacher talked about how, as we go through life, we often look forward to "another time," and it starts when we're little children wanting to be big kids. Then we want to get our driver's license, then to graduate, find a partner, have a family, and then to retire. "When," the preacher asked, "do we stop and say, 'This, *this* is the day'"?

That sermon was so memorable for me as I sat there listening because I was waiting for my then-fiancé to be granted a visa so he could move to the United States, and we could begin our life together. Each day seemed to last forever, and I just wanted to fly past all the waiting so my life could begin. As I sat there listening, I pondered what it might mean to claim, truly, *"This is the day the LORD has made."* Fellow traveller, *today* is the day, the one right before you now.

God of yesterday, today, and tomorrow, I give you thanks for this day before me. This is the day you have made, and I will rejoice and be glad in it.

Razzies and Oscars

Read Psalm 30:4–5.

Weeping may linger for the night,
But joy comes with the morning. (v. 5)

My husband and I love watching movies, and Sandra Bullock is one of our favorite actresses. Though she has played many roles, she often gets cast as a likable, friendly person; it seems her personality is like that in real life too.

A while ago, Sandra Bullock was awarded—and accepted—a Golden Raspberry award. The Golden Raspberry, affectionately called a "Razzie," is basically the opposite of an Oscar, given to performances that are deemed phenomenally bad for one reason or another. Sandra Bullock received hers for her work in *All About Steve*. In her acceptance speech, she was funny and received the award with humor.

And then something amazing happened. The very next day Sandra Bullock was awarded an Oscar for Best Actress for her work in *The Blind Side*. In her acceptance speech she said, "I have so many people to thank for my good fortune in this lifetime, and this is a once-in-a-lifetime experience, I know."

It occurs to me that our lives, and especially our Christian journey, are very much like that. We receive both Razzie awards and Oscar awards, and sometimes they happen in the same weekend. Life can be a wild ride, but we know that Jesus is our constant companion in all the highest highs and lowest lows. The important part is to show up for all of it, to accept our Razzies along with our Oscars.

God of mountain tops and valleys, draw near to me in the Razzie moments of life and make me humble in the Oscar moments. Thank you for your grace and faithfulness through it all.

Beauty

Read Psalm 27:4.

...to behold the beauty of the LORD
and to inquire in [God's] temple. (v. 4b)

Joshua Bell is a world-famous violinist who plays to crowds that pay expensive prices to listen to his work. He was a child prodigy. To hear him play will send shivers up your spine, his fans say.

One time he was involved in an interesting experiment. What if he wore regular street clothes instead of a tuxedo and played his $3.5 million-dollar violin for free in a Washington D.C. subway station? Would people stop and notice? Would crowds gather? Would scores of music lovers stop to listen? Several people predicted that Bell's playing would stop the foot traffic cold. After all, this is a man of world-renowned fame, a man with unmatched talent.

What happened is not surprising, but it is incredibly humbling: no crowds gathered. Traffic didn't stop. Bell walked away with a total of thirty-seven dollars in his violin case, mostly from folks who threw the money in the case and ran away quickly. A few people did stop to listen, but they were the exception, not the rule. By and large, folks hurried past and treated him as if he were invisible.

Isn't this how we often go through life? Amazing things are happening, right under our noses, but we don't see them. We don't stop to notice. We rush past. How can we take the time to savor the priceless treasures God puts in our path each and every day?

God of every day, thank you for the beauty and wonder all around me. Help me to slow down and enjoy it.

Sacrifice

Read Romans 5:6–11.

Rarely will anyone die for a righteous person—though perhaps for a good person someone might actually dare to die. But God proves his love for us in that while we still were sinners Christ died for us. (vv. 7–8)

Cameron Lyle was a track and field star for the University of New Hampshire. When he was 21, he learned that he was a bone-marrow match for a 21-year-old cancer patient. The procedure requires being poked in the hip hundreds of times. After the procedure, patients need about a month of recovery. Cameron learned that donating his bone marrow to the cancer patient would effectively end his college track and field career.

Cameron said there was only one choice: to donate. To compete in the shot put a few times or to save someone's life was an easy choice for him, but it also was a sacrificial choice. It must have been difficult for him to walk away from a career where he was enjoying great success; I imagine there was also great joy in realizing what he was gaining.

As Christians we use the language of sacrifice when we talk about what happened with Christ on the cross. When we sacrifice, we give up something, be it opportunity or time or money. We often find it easier to sacrifice for those we love: family members, close friends. In what ways do we have the opportunity to sacrifice for those who are strangers to us yet might depend on us for their very lives? There is joy in sacrifice and sharing because it makes us more like Christ, our Savior.

God of service and sacrifice, help me to be more like your son, Jesus, by giving sacrificially. Amen.

Gardens

Read: Mark 4:3–9.

"Other seed fell into good soil and brough forth grain." (v. 8a)

My mom's gardening method is easy to learn. Step one: gather a handful of seeds. Step two: toss the seeds on empty soil. Step three: wait. That's it. My husband's gardening method, on the other hand, is a lot harder to learn. It has way more than three steps, and it involves a lot of digging and pruning, shaping, and careful watering. Though I've never heard it, I suspect he also talks and sings to his plants, just to make sure that they are well loved and cared for.

Both my mom and my husband have beautiful gardens. My mom is sometimes amazed at the types of flowers that bloom, despite the fact that she paid very little attention to them. My husband is sometimes disappointed when his flowers die, despite his best efforts. In the end, both my mom and my husband have learned something valuable about God through gardening: it doesn't depend only on them.

We do well to remember this when we are cultivating relationships with others and with God. Sometimes relationships bloom and grow effortlessly and at other times, even when we work extraordinarily hard, they fail. Often we are forced to step back and admit that there are things we don't know about what makes a relationship bloom.

God of rain and drought, help me to be content in the knowledge that there is an element of mystery in my relationships. Help me to trust in you to provide the growth that is needed in my life.

I Love You Big

Read 1 Corinthians 13.

And the greatest of these is love. (v. 13b)

It didn't take long for my sons to learn that the response to "I love you" is "I love you too." The toddler-sized pun is inevitable: "I love you three!" My son Clayton loves to respond to "I love you." We even made up an "I love you" game. I say something like "I love you circle!" and he responds "I love you square!"

"I love you red!"

"I love you orange!"

"I love you trains!"

"I love you taxis!"

One day I gave Clayton a hug and a kiss good night and said, "I love you."

He responded, "I love you Colombian food."

It was heartwarming for this simple reason: Clayton loves Colombian food. He loves eating the arepa and the *chicharrón* and the *arroz*. He loves *pollo a la plancha* and *jugo de mango*. It's not just the food he loves; he loves the experience of going to the Colombian restaurant and chatting with the owner and the waiters. Colombian food is, for Clayton, pure joy.

Though it's difficult to interpret what might be in the heart of a toddler, it seemed to me that "I love you Colombian food" might just be the three-year-old equivalent of "I love you a whole lot."

God loves us not only red and orange and trains and taxis, God loves us Colombian food too!

God of extravagant love, thank you for loving us in ways that are all-encompassing and full of joy. Help us to love one another with the same extravagant love.

Everywhere You Go

Read Ruth 1:15–17.

"Where you go, I will go;
where you lodge, I will lodge." (v. 16b)

Two sisters in my congregation Dorothy* and Mabel* lived together in their old age. Both were in the ninth decade of life, and they had come back together after living separate lives for many years. Though they lived apart for much of the time between childhood and old age, their bond became one of the strongest I've ever seen. Where Dorothy would go, Mabel would go and vice versa. In fact, when Mabel would end up in the hospital for some type of health complication—wouldn't you know it?—Dorothy would march into the doctor's office insisting that her cold was "probably pneumonia" and insisting, "You'd better get me admitted into the hospital to get it checked out."

Perhaps Dorothy genuinely thought her cough was pneumonia and should be checked out, but we became a little suspicious when, a few months later, Mabel was in the hospital again, and Dorothy swore up and down "My hip is really sore. I could hardly get out of bed yesterday and today. Oh, and I've been having heart palpitations." Back to the hospital she went, with her sister.

It makes me wonder what it looks like to be unabashedly faithful to another person, whether the relationship is that of parent and child, spouses, friends, or, as Dorothy and Mabel demonstrated, sisters. We worship a faithful God who is present where we are. "Where you go, I will go."

Faithful God, you are present in the dark and light places of life's journey. Help me to ponder and consider what it means to be faithful to the ones I love.

*Names changed in respect of parishioners' privacy.

Communicating with God

Read Matthew 7:7–11.

"How much more will your Father in heaven give good things to those who ask him!" (v. 11b)

One of the funny things about communication that my son Clayton has taught me is that talking and communicating are not the same thing. This became abundantly clear when Clayton learned to say, "Where is it?" He learned that "Where is it?" had something to do with finding that which was lost, but he didn't learn that you have to have a common understanding with your communication partner of what "it" is. Thus, he would look at me inquisitively and sweetly ask, "Mama, where is it?" I would offer a sympathetic look and say, "Where is what, darling?" to which he simply repeated, "Where is it?"

Several times this dance went around, gradually escalating each time until Clayton was face-down on the rug crying, "Where is iiiiiiiiiiiiiiiiiiiiiiiiiiit!" It was hard to see him frustrated, but as I watched the whole scene unfold, I realized how often this happens in the adult world. We want to communicate something to someone, but we don't have the right information to speak in a way so that the other person will hear us and understand us.

I wonder if this happens between God and God's people. Is it possible that we might be trying to communicate to God in ways that seem to God as silly as Clayton's "Where is it?" seemed to me?

When we are trying to comprehend the mystery of prayer, why don't we seem to hear answers to the questions we are asking God? Perhaps we simply don't know everything we need to know. Not yet, anyway.

God of mystery and unanswered prayer, help me to rest in the truth that we know much less than we need to know when it comes to understanding all there is to know. Amen.

That Which Is Near

Read Isaiah 43:16–19.

I am about to do a new thing. (v. 19a)

Many of us have seen the same scene, either in person or in a photograph: a man or woman, usually with a scowl on his or her face, standing outside with a large sign. The sign says, "Repent! The end is near!" or simply "The end is near!" I don't know about you, but that scene usually unnerves me. For many reasons. My chief reason for disliking signs like that is that the message is one of fear. The idea is that passersby will worry so much about the world coming to an end and the state of their eternal souls that they'll make a snap decision for a faithful life. I'm always perplexed that so many people find this to be an effective, meaningful way to reach strangers with a message.

If you had a message to put on a sign for the entire world to see, what would it say?

Recently I saw a photo of two smiling men holding a sign that read, "The beginning is near." Because it stood in such sharp contrast to the message that "the end is near" and because the two were smiling so broadly, it filled my day with hope. All day I thought about how the beginning was near in my life: the beginning of good things that are just on the horizon, the beginning of joy and hope and peace in my life and the lives of those to whom I minister.

Friends, the beginning is near for you too. What is just now beginning in your life?

God of new beginnings, help me to embrace a message of joy and beginning rather than doom and death. This is the message you have given to your world. Amen.

What Is Your Name?

Read Psalm 139:13–18.

Your eyes beheld my unformed substance. (v. 16a)

I love to ask people the stories of their names. "How did you come to get your name? Were you named after someone, or is there a story involved?" Rarely do people answer no. Some people have simple answers: "My parents just liked the sound of it"; others have more circuitous answers: "My dad was a schoolteacher and was always vetoing the names that my mom wanted to use, so this was one of the few names they could agree on."

We get our names because the people naming us have very specific thoughts about the new life that is about to enter the world and make a mark on the planet. We are named after meaningful people or beloved songs or movies. Sometimes we get names that sound pretty when rolling off the tongue. Some people are named after saints, others after pop stars. Some people name their children popular names that are at the peak of trendiness and familiarity. Others choose a name that is deliberately unique and one of a kind, so that their child might stand out.

When we are named we become someone distinct and unique in the world. We are known; we are named. Psalm 139 has very much to say about how we are known intimately to God. The psalmist talks about how every single hair on our heads is known and counted by God. We were knit together by God, unique in God's eyes.

Do you know the story of your name? Whatever the story and regardless of whether you know that story, take comfort in knowing that the God of creation sees you as unique and individual. You are one of a kind.

God of many names, help me to know and internalize my own uniqueness. Help me always to remember that I am one of a kind.

Do You Believe in Luck?

Read 1 Thessalonians 5:12–22.

Give thanks in all circumstances; for this is the will of God in Christ Jesus for you. (v. 18)

When I was first learning to speak Spanish, I received an internship in Honduras. On my first day of work, I asked my host family how to get there. "Cualquier bus," they said. "Any bus." Just to make sure, I repeated it, "Really? Any bus?" "Yes," they insisted. Any bus could take me straight to my destination. In fact, all the buses that passed by our main street went in the same direction as my work.

Once I boarded the bus, imagine my surprise (and a little terror) when the bus driver turned onto a different road. Somehow I was at the wrong place at the wrong time and boarded the one bus that transported passengers to the local university. The bus rambled on for what seemed like eternity before I was finally able to tell my story to some strangers who helped me get back to where I needed to be. Words cannot express how grateful I was for their kind assistance.

At the end of the evening, I told the story to my host family. They were mortified.

"Traci, the chances that the one bus that went a different way would stop at that particular bus stop at the exact moment you were there is unbelievable!"

Many times Christians talk about being blessed and fortunate about narrowly escaping tragedy because of God's good provision and faithfulness. The truth is, however, God is with us all the time, even when we experience life's adverse situations, when the unbelievable and unfortunate things happen, and when we are inconvenienced or lost. In those moments we can rely on the kindness of strangers to help us find our way.

God of it all, you are with us when we narrowly escape tragedy, but you are also with us when we are victims of unfortunate circumstances, too. Help us to see your hand in all things. Amen.

Daily Bread

Read Matthew 6:9–13.

"Give us this day our daily bread." (v. 11)

My congregation recently had the opportunity to pack more than 15,000 meals for an organization called Stop Hunger Now. The meals are prepackaged with mostly rice, a vitamin packet, some dehydrated vegetables, and seasonings. The food in the packets wouldn't count for a meal in my North American context, but I am well aware of the life-sustaining power these small servings of rice contain. We later learned that the meals we packed were sent to Haiti, the poorest country in the western hemisphere, a country where half the children are malnourished by age five.

When I helped our mission committee and others organize the event, I was not prepared for the intense personal feelings of spiritual connection I felt toward the people receiving the meals. As the cups of rice whooshed through the funnels and the vitamin packets were added to the bags, I began to remember the words of the Lord's Prayer "Give us this day our daily bread." It was overwhelming to see bags of rice filled and packed and stacked, over and over again. It took a semi truck to haul them all away.

Many people around the globe are not guaranteed their next meal; they long and wait and pray for it. Answers for how to make sure that everyone on earth has enough to eat are complex, and there are many different opinions and ideas about how Christians might be faithful in looking for a solution. One thing is sure, though: Lent is a time for prayer, fasting, and almsgiving. Might it also be a time for us to pray, fast, and give our alms for those who need daily bread? I think so.

God of food and hunger, help us to reflect on what we can do to help the most vulnerable in our world. As we pray for spiritual bread, may we remember to pray for literal bread as well. Amen.

Risk

Read Matthew 28:16–20.

"Go therefore and make disciples of all nations." (v. 19a)

One day, my mentor and friend was telling me about new ground she was breaking at work. She was in the middle of a risky, complicated initiative that had the potential either to fall flat on its face or change the industry in which she works. No pressure! I was asking a lot of questions and she said, "You know, I really don't know. I'm going to be building the plane while I fly it."

I've since learned that people say that all the time, that it's not a new phrase, and that she certainly didn't invent it, yet it was the first time I had ever heard it. I love that phrase. I had the image of my friend in the cockpit flying her plane and simultaneously building the body around her. It described the situation perfectly: risky, but with the opportunity for huge payoff. If she does it well, she'll be flying to new territory.

I wonder if we, as the church, would be served by building the plane while we fly it, by taking risks and daring to go places others haven't gone before.

This is certainly true of the Great Commission. We are to go to the *ends of the earth* to bring the good news of the gospel of Jesus Christ to all we encounter. I can't imagine that traveling to the ends of the earth is a command that Jesus intended to be safe and easy. When Jesus talked about the ends of the earth, I have a feeling he meant places like prisons we'd rather not visit, mental hospitals that are scary and uncomfortable, retirement homes where folks sit largely abandoned. The gospel message takes us to places our plane is not equipped to fly. If we want to make it to the ends of the earth, we're going to need a new plane, and we might have to build it ourselves.

God of innovation and risk, help me to be brave as I travel to places I've never been before. Give me strength and courage as I follow your call.

Feed the People

Read Ephesians 4:1–6.

Lead a life worthy of the calling to which you have been called. (v. 1b)

"I'm going to give you some advice," my mentor said when I was learning about ministry.

"Preaching every week is like feeding the people. That's your job. You feed the people. Sometimes they get roast beef and mashed potatoes, and sometimes it's peanut butter and jelly and water. But if they eat and they're not hungry when they leave, you've done your job. Just make sure it's not peanut butter and jelly every week, or you'll be in trouble."

I've taken that advice to heart and shared it with other ministers and friends over the years. It's become a running joke in my family too. On an important day like Easter, my parents will call and say, "Oh, I bet you gave them a nice ham and potatoes this morning, didn't you, Traci!" If I've had a week with a couple of memorial services and a sick child, I might confess to my mom, "It felt like a ham and cheese sandwich. And not even that good ham, either. The cheap kind." Good parent that she is, my mom always assures me that next week I'll have the time and energy to serve up something a lot more appealing.

My mentor's advice applies not just to preachers of the Word, but to listeners as well. When we hear messages or sermons that we don't particularly like, we might do very well to ask ourselves, "Was it food?" God's truth comes to us in ways that may be palatable and luxurious one time, yet bland and not quite our style the next. Sometimes the teachers and preachers in our lives give us steamed vegetables when we were hoping for chocolate. It's all food for the journey.

God of the feast and the simple meal, help me to be sustained and nourished on my way. May I focus on the sustenance that will give me strength for the journey. Amen.

Listen with Your Heart

Read Colossians 3:12–14.

Above all, clothe yourselves with love, which binds everything together in perfect harmony. (v. 14)

I learned once that the Chinese character for "to listen," transliterated ting, comprises the symbols of four other words: *ears, eyes, undivided attention,* and *heart.* When I reflect on what it means to communicate with another person, to hear and to be heard, it makes perfect sense that the Chinese symbol would be thorough enough to include all the symbols of the senses involved in being a good listener.

This message was brought home to me loudly and clearly when I was in college, an era before iPads, e-readers, and smartphones. I had a trusted mentor, Bruce, who ran a successful business. Bruce often juggled many tasks at the same time, and one afternoon I stopped by his office to see if he could offer some advice on a paper I was writing. As I sat in front of his desk, explaining my paper proposal, his phone (you know, the kind with a cord!) rang. And it rang again. And then it rang a third time.

"Aren't you going to get that?" I asked.

"Why? I'm talking to you," was his simple reply.

That was more than sixteen years ago, and I'm still talking about it. I will never forget it. When I think of Bruce, it's one of the first things I think about: *"I'm talking to you."*

One of the gifts God gives us during the season of Lent is the gift to be reflective, to consider where God would have us repent, turn around, and go a different direction. Might it be that God is asking us to repent of the many ways we are so casual with our listening? Perhaps God is asking us to devote heart, eyes, ears, and undivided attention to others, as we truly listen to them.

God of our speaking and our hearing, help me to be a better listener to you and those around me. Forgive me for my divided attention.

Peekaboo! I See You!

Read Jeremiah 23:23–24.

*Who can hide in secret places so that I cannot see them? says the LORD.
(v. 24a)*

It's the first game many of us ever played. Child-development experts and psychologists have noticed an endearing fact about children and hiding, and it's readily apparent to any grandpa, auntie, or other loved one who has played peekaboo with a very young child: when children cover their eyes, they think you can't see them. If I can't see you, you can't see me, their logic goes. Even children as old as four years old often still believe that a puppet can "hide" by covering his eyes.

As children grow older and learn to play hide-and-seek, they still cover their eyes while they're hiding. They also often make silly mistakes where they "hide" in plain view. Many fascinating psychology studies about this phenomenon have been conducted, but essentially they boil down to this: young children make a distinction between being seen physically (their bodies) and being seen on a deeper level (their selves).* Research supports the idea that young children believe that two people can't see each other unless their eyes meet.

I wonder about the spiritual implications of it all. We often act like young children in God's eyes. We think that we're doing a good job of hiding from God when we're really just covering our eyes. God sees right through our childish denial to the deepest parts of us. We can't hide.

God of the visible and the invisible, forgive me for trying to hide from you. Help me to see and be seen. Amen.

*Summary of hiding behavior research: http://bps-research-digest.blogspot. com/2012/10/why-do-children-hide-by-covering-their.html .

Heavy Arms

Read Matthew 11:28–30.

"Come to me, all you that are weary and are carrying heavy burdens, and I will give you rest." (v. 28)

My three-year-old is learning how to dress himself, and it's often entertaining to watch. Mismatched clothes are just the beginning. There are shirts on backwards (and upside down!), out-of-season clothes proudly worn in public, and the robot shirt every day of the week if he can get away with it.

A few weeks ago as he was struggling to get out of a T-shirt, grunting and straining, I asked, "Do you need help?"

"NO!"

"Okay."

He continued to struggle for a few minutes until he gave up, looking me straight in the eyes.

"My arm is too heavy, Mama," he said.

It was such an endearing, cute thing to say, but my eyes welled up at the sound of those words: "My arm is too heavy." Watching him struggle and hearing him articulate this idea that his arm was "too heavy" made me think of all the burdens and struggles he'll face throughout his life. I thought of the many burdens and struggles I've had in my life. Sometimes our arms really are too heavy.

"My yoke is easy and my burden is light," Jesus says.

In what ways and when do we turn our burdens over to Christ, acknowledging that they are too heavy for us to bear on our own?

God of grace, thank you for the charge and challenge to release our burdens to you. Help us truly let them go, that we might be free.

Who Made You?

Read Isaiah 45:9–19.

Woe to those who quarrel with their Maker. . . . Does the clay say to the potter, "What are you making?" (v. 9, NIV).

At first glance, this seems like a fairly harsh verse. ("Woe to those" tends to do that to a verse!) Digging deeper, however, this verse is about loving and honoring God by loving and honoring ourselves.

When we think of God as Creator, we often speak as if God is done with this creative work. It's almost as if God created the heavens, the earth, the stars, and the planets and then switched roles from "Creator" to "Observer." Isn't it true, however, that as God molds and shapes us into the people we're meant to be, God is still in the act of creating? The scriptural implication is that when we criticize, abuse, and neglect ourselves, we are quarreling with our Maker. Whether we intend to or not, when we hold ourselves in low esteem, we are essentially saying to God, "You aren't doing it right."

Of course, this is not to say that there isn't a place for true humility and repentance when we stray from God's plans for us. In my experience, however, folks tend to find it easier to bring themselves down than to build themselves up. Lent is a time for reflection and repentance. Let us repent of the ways in which we fail and the ways in which we do not live up to the ideals God and others have for us. In addition, let us repent of the ways in which we fail to recognize our own value and worth before God, our Maker. God made you and is making you. Does the clay say to the potter, "What are you making?"

God, our Maker, forgive me for selling myself short. Help me to recognize and honor you as my Creator all the days of my life. Amen.

Practicing Imagination

Read Joel 2:28–29.

Your sons and your daughters shall prophesy,
your old men shall dream dreams,
and your young men shall see visions. (v. 28b)

I read about a study that presented the following fascinating data*: if you tell an average four-year-old to stand perfectly still for as long as possible, he'll be able to do it for about a minute, on average. But if you tell the average four-year-old to pretend she's a soldier guarding a castle and that it's very important for her to remain as still as possible and not move even a muscle or else she'll be swallowed by dragons, she'll be able to do it for about four minutes. The difference? Imagination. There's nothing inspiring about standing still for a minute, especially if you're four years old. But guarding a castle! Now there's something anyone can get behind.

As I look around at Christians in worshiping communities in my city and world, I wonder if we haven't lost our sense of imagination sometimes. We tell ourselves to stand still, and we just can't do it. We need to tell ourselves that we're guarding castles, because we are.

I believe that imagination is a spiritual discipline, just like prayer, fasting, and almsgiving. As with any spiritual discipline, it takes practice and focus. Many people choose to take on an additional spiritual practice during Lent, and perhaps this has been your custom as well. How might you choose to foster the spiritual practice of imagination this Lent?

What will you do to foster your imagination this Lent?

God of imagination, thank you for surprising me. Help me to see you in new ways. Amen.

* *Study cited in Welcome to Your Child's Brain by Sandra Aamodt and Sam Wang.*

Hunger

Read John 6:35–40.

"I am the bread of life. Whoever comes to me will never be hungry, and whoever believes in me will never be thirsty." (v. 35b)

One communion Sunday we had a loaf of bread left over and the elders gave it to me to take home and make sandwiches for me and my family. I stuck it on the shelf, meaning to take it with me, and then promptly forgot. The next week on Wednesday, I forgot my lunch at home (forgetting things is a theme with me!) and about three o'clock, I was ravenously hungry.

I didn't want to break my work rhythm and go home or go out, so I started looking around the church for something to eat. The church fridge, usually a great source of cake, cookies, or other leftover (and unhealthy) treats was uncharacteristically bare, and my snack basket was empty. I poured myself another cup of coffee and sat back down at my desk, hoping that would do the trick. Then I saw the forgotten Communion loaf staring at me. I tore the bag open, ripped off a piece of bread, and started to eat, way too fast.

This may have been what Jesus had in mind when he said, "I am the bread of life." Though our communion celebrations with the tiny cubes of bread and itty-bitty shot glasses of juice are important symbols and reminders of the feast, they are approximations of something much deeper. When Jesus said he was the bread of life, he meant that he is there, waiting to fill our deepest hunger.

Ever-present God, thank you for giving us Jesus, the bread of life. Help us to seek him out to fill our deepest hunger each and every day. Amen.

Transformed

Read Psalm 30.

You have turned my mourning into dancing. (v. 11a)

The most incredible stories about garage sales I've ever heard have to do with people finding a treasure of immense value. This particular story about a garage sale is about the immense value of kindness and of transformation.

The woman hosting the garage sale had lost her unborn baby boy tragically to a fatal umbilical-cord condition that had deprived him of oxygen. She was selling many of the baby's things she had bought in preparation. Can you imagine the grief of selling all those items that symbolized her deceased child's unrealized hopes and dreams? It seems a pain almost too deep to bear.

One of the customers learned of the woman's grief and her tragic loss and asked about the baby crib in the garage. The crib wasn't for sale, but the customer convinced the grieving mother to sell it anyway.

A few weeks later the customer returned to the woman's home with a gift. He had transformed the crib into a beautiful bench for the bereft mother—a memorial for the child she didn't have a chance to watch grow up.

Nothing will ever take away this woman's grief or the sadness of everyone who had come to love the unborn baby boy. However, I'd like to believe that the kindness and intuition of that loving stranger may have helped them proclaim with the psalmist: "You have turned my mourning into dancing."

God of grief and despair, thank you for sending strangers to help bear our burdens with us when we are in the pits. Help us to lift each other up and provide encouragement to one another. Amen.

Together at the Grave

Read Genesis 25:7–9.

His sons Isaac and Ishmael buried him in the cave of Machpelah. (v. 9a)

The story of Isaac and Ishmael, as it is told in the Hebrew Scriptures, is a story about a broken relationship. Ishmael, Abraham's eldest son, has favor because he is a firstborn, but Isaac has favor because he is born of Sarah, Abraham's wife, whereas Ishmael was born of Hagar, a maidservant. The enmity between the two brothers ran deep. The Hebrew Scriptures do show one compelling instance, however, where Isaac and Ishmael are unified with a common purpose, at a place we read about in Genesis 25—Abraham's grave. Both sons come together and grieve the death of their father Abraham in the same place at the same time.

How many times have we seen this in our own families? Deep resentment and strife persist, right up until the day that a family member is dead and gone. Sometimes the reconciliation is lasting. After the bickering parties come together at the grave, they realize that their differences weren't as significant as they may have thought. Other times, though, even the death of a beloved family member is not enough to bring reconciliation and peace.

I wonder how Abraham might have felt if he had had the opportunity to be near his sons in life rather than death. What gift might we bring to our own families if we seek resolution and reconciliation today, rather than tomorrow?

God of Isaac and Ishmael, thank you for the gift of peace. Help me to be a peacemaker in my family, my community, and my world. Amen.

Patience

Read Romans 5:2–5.

Endurance produces character, and character produces hope, and hope does not disappoint us. (vv. 4–5a)

One of my professional areas of focus is ministry to children and families. I wrote a book about this topic, filled with many faith practices for families to use. One practice I included was designed to help families talk about what it means to wait for something that happens gradually or for something that takes a long time. Though it's a little more complicated than this, the basic idea is that families have to wait for water to evaporate from a glass.

The editor of the book hated it. To be fair, he didn't hate it, but he didn't love it either. He thought it was boring and recommended cutting it from the manuscript. I argued that the fact it was boring was *the entire point of the exercise.* It stayed in. I joked with the editor that I was assigning *him* to do the waiting exercise to learn to appreciate it. Even though he laughed, I don't think he ever took me up on that idea.

Isn't it interesting that the things we need to do the most are often the least appealing? The idea that we might discover how to be patient by waiting for water to evaporate from a glass seems simplistic and monotonous, but we can learn a lesson from the waiting for the passing by, each day wondering, "Will today be the day?" We know that eventually the glass will be empty, but the days of waiting and wondering drag on, and eventually we might even stop noticing the glass at all.

What are you waiting for? Maybe you will receive it all at one time, or maybe it will come bit by bit, molecule by molecule. Maybe one day you will remember to take notice, and the glass will be empty.

God of time, thank you for the gift of patience. Help me to remember that sometimes the transformation I am hoping for is coming to me slowly rather than all at once.

Unseen Hope

Read Romans 8:12–28.

Who hopes for what is seen? (v. 24b)

This stops me cold every time I read it: "Hope that is seen is no hope at all. Who hopes for what they already have?" (v. 24b, NIV). The statement is both obvious and obtuse all at the same time. Obviously we hope for something because we don't already have it. But want does it mean to hope for something unseen?

In Spanish the verb "to hope" is esperar. Esperar also means "to wait."

To hope for something, then, is to wait for it. This is exactly what Paul says in Romans 8. When we hope, we wait. Both these things—hoping and waiting—are hard. Sometimes the things we hope for don't come to us in this life, or if they do, they look very different from what we expected.

I heard a story that after 9/11, when the dogs were looking in the rubble for survivors, they became depressed because they didn't find anyone. In an effort to help them carry on, survivors hid in the rubble so the dogs would feel the success they needed to continue their difficult task.

That story is simultaneously hope-filled and hopeless. On the one hand, it illustrates the great power and perseverance of the human spirit. On the other hand, it is a reminder of the utter horror and dismay of that day.

The hope that we have in Christ is one that we will one day receive the things that we do not yet have, sometimes only after a great deal of waiting. Hope that is seen is no hope at all.

God of triumph and tragedy, thank you for the gift of hope. Help me wait patiently for that which is unseen. Amen.

Grace

Read Ephesians 2:4–10.

For by grace you have been saved through faith, and this is not your own doing; it is the gift of God. (v. 8)

"No matter how far down the wrong road you've gone, turn back." —Turkish proverb

I've given a children's message before about God's unconditional love. I say to the children, "Does God love you?" to which they all loudly and enthusiastically reply, "YES!" Then I say, "But what if you do something bad, does God love you then?" To this about half the children persevere and respond, "Yes, God loves you, even when you do something bad." I reaffirm that it's true: God really does love us, even when we do something bad. Then I say, "What if you do something really, really bad, something that makes you have to go to jail? What if you do something so bad that your mom and your dad and everybody in the whole world are disappointed in you? Does God love you even then?" At the third variation of the question, invariably there's silence, shaking of heads, or a resounding "No, God does not love you if you do something so bad that you go to jail."

Sadly, adults fall into the same trap, consciously or subconsciously. We might believe that God will forgive our petty sins, our white lies, our bad moments, but we have a really hard time internalizing that God completely forgives our worst moments, the horrible unforgivable things we've done to ourselves and others.

Though it is a time of introspection and repentance, Lent is also a season to reflect deeply on the fact that our sins are forgiven in Christ.

God of our failings and weaknesses, thank you that you forgive us for our sins, even when we are slow to forgive ourselves. Help us to rest in the knowledge that we are a new creation. Amen.

Standing on the Wings

Read Exodus 14:21–31.

Thus the Lord saved Israel that day. (v. 30a)

Predictably, when I'm leading a Bible study on some of the amazing miracle stories told in the Old and New Testaments, someone will ask a variation on the question "Why doesn't God do those kinds of miracles now?" Others in the group will often explain that God's miracles are now smaller things that we experience every day, like a sunset or a newborn baby. I like that answer, but I don't think it gets to the heart of the question. The heart of the question really is "Why doesn't God do flashy, large-scale miracles like the parting of the Red Sea now, as God did in biblical times?" My answer: God does do those kinds of miracles now.

One such miracle occurred in 2010, when Sully Sullenberger landed a plane on the Hudson River, and everybody lived. I don't care what anybody says; it was a divine miracle of God, without question. I love everything about that story. I love that the people evacuated onto the wings until help arrived. I love that the pilot, Captain Sullenberger, said that he didn't pray, because he assumed that everybody in the back had that covered. What I love most is that when he was asked if he worried about whether or not the landing would be successful, he said, "I knew I could do it." Tell me, where does that type of assurance come from?

Just like I do with the miracle stories in the Old and New Testaments, I come back to the story of the plane landing on the Hudson several times a year. Each time I watch the YouTube video of the captain's interview on 60 Minutes and each time I cry tears of joy, giving thanks to God for such an amazing miracle. God still performs miracles. Believe it!

God of miracles, thank you for continuing to perform miracles right before our very eyes. Help us to notice them. Amen.

Eleven Words

Read Philippians 4:8–9.

Finally, beloved, whatever is true, whatever is honorable, whatever is just, whatever is pure, whatever is pleasing, whatever is commendable, if there is any excellence and if there is anything worthy of praise, think about these things. (v. 8)

Day in and day out, hospice workers sit at the bedsides of men and women who are making their final journey from this life into the world to come. In my experience, many of them have been given great gifts of kindness, intuition, and compassion.

I heard an interview by an end-of-life expert who said that there are eleven words that people most need to say or to hear at the end of life: "Please forgive me. I forgive you. I love you. Thank you." Wrapped up in those eleven words is the whole of our human experience, and at the end of life, when everything we've done and lived and believed comes into very sharp focus, those eleven words have meaning.

The interviewer reminded me of a prophet urging repentance when he pointed out that most of us need to do some work on those words now and not wait until the final moments when this life is fading away into obscurity. How will you walk through the eleven words as you finish your Lenten journey this year? Will you say "Please forgive me" to someone you have damaged or wounded? Will you say "I forgive you" to someone in need of your mercy and grace? Will you say "I love you" to someone again or for the first time? Will you say "Thank you" to your loved ones and to God for the many good gifts in your life? Don't wait. Do it today.

Gracious, loving, and forgiving God, thank you for these eleven words that bring so many things so sharply into focus. Help us to have the courage we need to say them out loud today. Amen.

Healing Waters

Read John 5:1–9.

"Sir, I have no one to put me into the pool when the water is stirred up."
(v. 7a)

The scripture for today is a fairly straightforward story of healing. A man who is unable to walk is sitting by a pool. He calls out to Jesus and asks to be made well. Jesus heals him, and he gets up and walks away. The detail that always moves me in this story happens when the man says to Jesus, "There is nobody to carry me down to the water."

The pool supposedly had healing properties. Some believe the waters were a sort of mineral bath or natural hot springs. People with all sorts of ailments would go down to the waters to receive healing. Those who couldn't walk had to be carried down.

The man points out that he has nobody to carry him down to the waters. As I read those words, I'm filled with compassion for a person who could see the healing waters and who wanted them, yet who needed help to get them.

I wonder about our churches, our healing pools of grace. Are there people who are sitting around our edges wanting to be dipped into the waters, if only they had help? Do we walk by them on our way down, receiving healing for ourselves but leaving other people out?

This Lenten season, as you have journeyed through a time of personal reflection, healing, and wholeness, is anybody watching you who needs those blessings too? Is there anyone you can carry gently down to the waters as well, that they might receive God's grace?

God of healing and wholeness, thank you for being with me on this Lenten journey. Help me to take the lessons I've been learning and share them with others as well.

Peach Pie

Read 1 John 3:1–3.

See what love the Father has given us, that we should be called children of God. (v. 1)

I'm not sure when, but at some point before I was too old (but old enough to be entrusted with the stove), I set about the process of making a peach pie. I'm not sure exactly what possessed me to make a peach pie from scratch, with very limited knowledge of pie-making in general, but I went about it anyway. Predictably, it didn't turn out very well. I don't remember all of the elements of what went wrong, but I do remember having to serve it in bowls with spoons instead of with plates and forks. I'm sure this wasn't the pie's only failing.

What I do remember, though—very clearly—is my dad's reaction.

"So delicious, Traci!" he said, "And you made it!"

When I pointed out that it was soupy and not at all what I intended it to be, he said, "Yes, but you made it. How many people can make a peach pie?"

What a lovely and apt example of God's great love for us. Though we might try and fail, God sees through to our hearts and our intentions. Had I not felt encouraged and loved in that moment, I might not have been as willing to continue learning to bake and cook new things.

Where are you on your journey of learning and discovery? Do you feel like your offerings are often subpar and soupy? Take heart that God loves and accepts you fully and completely.

God of our successes and our failures, thank you for loving us and accepting us when we don't live up to everything we have in mind. Help us to accept others with the same care and grace.

Donkey Fetchers

Read Mark 11:1–11.

He sent two of his disciples and said to them, "Go into the village ahead of you, and immediately as you enter it, you will find tied there a colt that has never been ridden." (vv. 1b–2a)

Thomas Long introduced the phrase "donkey fetcher" into my vocabulary in reference to this Palm Sunday story. Rev. Long talks about Jesus' triumphal entry into Jerusalem from the perspective of the disciples.

In the gospels, there's considerable discussion about where to find the colt and the donkey for Jesus, as well as how to untie them and what to do if someone questions them in the process. What odd duties for the disciples to carry out that day. I doubt they woke up that morning thinking, "I wonder what I'll be doing today? I bet I'll be going to borrow a donkey from a stranger for the LORD." They were donkey fetchers that day, and in their obedience they found that they were part of the amazing story of Jesus' entry into Jerusalem. The donkey is essential to the story. If the disciples had balked at their instructions, or refused them, or passed them on, the story would have been significantly different.

The thought begs the question "What sort of 'donkey fetching' is the LORD calling you to do?" What strange, unexpected, onerous task is facing you today? Will you accept the challenge of going forward and following through even if you aren't sure exactly what it means and what good will come of it?

As we move into this Holy Week—one of the holiest weeks of the year for Christians—let us enter in to it with a sense of service and obedience, looking for the many ways in which God will gently call us to service in God's kingdom.

God of duties great and small, thank you for the example and obedience of the disciples. Help me to be a "donkey fetcher" this week, whatever that means. Amen.

Cleaning House

Read Matthew 21:12–14.

Then Jesus entered the temple and drove out all who were selling and buying in the temple, and he overturned the tables of the money changers and the seats of those who sold doves. (v. 12)

On Monday Jesus clears out the temple. "You have made my father's house into a place for thieves," (or whatever) he says. Jesus is angry in this passage, violent. There is no way to sugarcoat that reality. Jesus in the temple isn't docile and gentle, patting the heads of children who sit lovingly on his knee. He's mad. Furious, even.

As we start our journey of Holy Week, pastors and priests, contemplatives, and devotionals often call us to be quiet and reflective, to go inside and undercover. What if, instead, we got mad? What if we got angry this Holy Week about all that is wrong with the world? Jesus shows us what it means to have a holy fury (often softened into "a righteous indignation.") When we hear about mass hunger and war and human rights violations in our world, a right response might be a holy fury. We have the right (and perhaps even the obligation) to turn over the tables when we read of the sale of children into sexual slavery, robbing them of any opportunity for a normal and happy childhood. We have the right (and perhaps even the obligation) to turn over the tables when our rivers and streams are full of trash or when hatred and oppression snuff out the voices of love and freedom.

Think differently about what it means to observe this Holy Week faithfully. Take some time to think about what makes you angry. Where is your holy fury? What tables need to be turned over?

God of joy and anger, thank you for reminding us that there is a time and a place for a holy fury in our lives. Help me to be angered by the things that anger you. Amen.

Betrayal

Read Luke 22:3–6.

So he consented and began to look for an opportunity to betray him to them when no crowd was present. (v. 6)

On Tuesday, Judas agrees to betray Jesus. This is the day he negotiates with the Sanhedrin. As I reflect on Judas's story, I wonder about what might have been going on in his mind between Tuesday and Friday. When we are reminded that Judas made plans to betray Jesus on Friday, we must remember that Judas's actions were premeditated and calculated. There is really no room to think that perhaps Judas was merely caught up in the last minute. He made plans for evil. He made plans to betray his (and our) savior and to turn him over to the authorities who would torture and kill him.

We can easily point the finger at Judas, but Scripture also reminds us that none of us is without fault: "All have sinned and fall short of the glory of God" (Romans 3:23). Introspection may not be a pleasant exercise, but we must remember that Lent is a time for us to look deep within our souls, that we might be brought back to full reconciliation with God.

Our story doesn't have to end the same way for us that it did for Judas. For us, it is still Tuesday. We still have time to change our minds about the evil we may be planning for Friday, or Saturday, or next week, or next year. We always have the opportunity to stop, make a course correction, and go another way.

Will you accept the invitation this day, this Tuesday, to change your course and go a new way?

Gracious and loving God, thank you for the spirit of discernment you have put into each of our hearts. When we feel that we're going in the wrong way, make us brave enough to change course. Amen.

Silence

Read Psalm 46.

Be still and know that I am God. (v. 10a)

Scripture is silent about what happens to Jesus and the disciples on this day. We can only guess. Maybe they were exhausted from the money-changing incident in the temple on Monday and the flurry of activity on Palm Sunday. Maybe they gathered together to talk about what was happening or what might happen in the days to come. Maybe Jesus found out about Judas's betrayal and thought about how he might address it. We don't know. It's quiet.

Perhaps Scripture's silence on this day is one way of inviting us to be silent today as well.

Silence in our culture is becoming ever more rare. Some of the most profound "noise" we deal with today is the blare of electronics. It's not so much the literal noise—although our electronics do have their share of buzzing and beeping—it's the noise of attention-stealing. We need to check our email, look at that text message, ask Google that burning question about how long to cook the chicken. It's a loud, persistent way to prevent us from having any semblance of stillness in our thoughts. Many of us realize this and we try, often unsuccessfully, to turn it off and keep silence for a period of time—a week, a day, an afternoon, an hour, even fifteen minutes. Even just fifteen minutes of undivided attention to someone or something that doesn't involve any outside electronics chatter is difficult to accomplish.

The key is not to try to do it alone. Find a friend or a family member who is committed to keeping the noise of electronics and gadgets at a minimum. Ask him or her to commit to a time of quiet and see where it takes you.

God of silence, thank you for the gift of a clear mind and an unburdened heart. Give us communities that we can trust to help us quiet the noise of distraction today. Amen.

Sacred Fellowship

Read Luke 22:7–23.

"I have eagerly desired to eat this Passover with you before I suffer." (v. 15)

This day, Thursday, is the last time the disciples are all together before Jesus' crucifixion. It is the day that Jesus breaks bread, lifts up the cup, and says the familiar words remembered by Christians every time they also gather together with bread and wine: "Do this in remembrance of me." I imagine it was a warm and intimate time for the disciples as they gathered there. I imagine that it might have been like some of the best dinner parties I've attended with close friends. A meal shared with friends bonded by a common experience is a treasure. With close friends you can dive deep and cry together, or share belly laughs and inside jokes. I wonder if the disciples joked and laughed at the Last Supper. Surely it wasn't a serious affair the whole time, from start to finish, was it?

In the hindsight of what happened the very next day—Jesus' arrest, torture, and crucifixion—that meal becomes even more meaningful and significant.

Let us take this lesson to heart the next time we are gathered around a holy table with our closest friends. Let us take a moment to remember that these moments of sharing and eating and enjoying one another are not always permanent. Let us remember to savor the good, close times with our loved ones, to treat them with respect and not tarnish them with our petty disagreements and worries.

God of sacred fellowship, thank you for the holy meals you have given to me. Help me to honor them and keep them holy. Amen.

The Worst Day in the Christian Year?

Read Luke 23:32–34.

Then Jesus said, "Father forgive them; for they do not know what they are doing." (v. 34)

Though it is called Good Friday, today is, in many ways, the worst day in the Christian year. This is the day we remember everything about Jesus' awful arrest, torture, crucifixion, and death. Today is the day we remember that he was betrayed by every single one of his closest friends. Today is the day we remember that Jesus was stripped of all of his clothes, mocked, spit upon, made to carry his own cross, and beaten until he could barely walk. We remember today that Jesus was nailed to a cross, that his side was pierced with a spear. We remember that he suffered in great, unimaginable ways. There is nothing good about this day—or is there?

When we read this passage, we cannot avoid noticing the very first thing Jesus says as he embarks upon his terror-filled journey: "Father, forgive them, for they do not know what they are doing" (v. 34).

When we read the gruesome and bloody details of what happened on that day, we are struck, time and again, with details of how violent the passage is. We must be very clear about one thing: this story is violent because people are violent. Contrast the actions of the soldiers and the crowd with the words of Jesus, which are words of forgiveness and grace: "They do not know what they are doing." Truer words were never spoken. The reason today is called Good Friday is that the forgiveness extended to us as human beings, undeserving as we are, is very good news.

God of forgiveness, thank you for the humbling example of grace and mercy that Jesus shows to his worst enemies. Help us to learn to be forgiving as well. Amen.

One Hundred Pounds

Read John 19:38–42.

They took the body of Jesus and wrapped it with the spices in linen cloths, according to the burial custom of the Jews. (v. 40)

Saturday is the day that Jesus is laid in the tomb. The Gospel of John tells us that Nicodemus and Joseph of Arimathea wrap Jesus' body with spices and aloe in strips of linen. When I read the story recently, there was a detail that stood out to me. Nicodemus brought one hundred pounds of myrrh and aloes to Jesus' grave to prepare him for burial. I don't know why, but I have always imagined Jesus' burial preparation as sort of ethereal and quiet. However, when I think about one hundred pounds of spices plus the linens, I realize that these two were carrying a lot of weight to the grave. The preparation surely must have been very physical with a lot of sweating, as they carried the spices and Jesus' body to the tomb.

We don't have many details about what might have been going through the men's minds as they performed this difficult and heartbreaking chore. I wonder if Nicodemus flashed back to the time when he asked Jesus what it took to inherit eternal life. Did he remember Jesus' words that he must be born again? Did the words take on new meaning as he wrapped Jesus' body in cloths and covered his skin in spices and ointment? My instinct tells me that whatever epiphany Nicodemus experienced about his spiritual journey with Jesus in the flesh was confirmed and made even more profound as he worked so intimately with Jesus in his death.

Facing death is a heavy burden. Confronting it is hard work. Still, we can learn lessons from it, right there in the tomb.

God of life and of death, thank you for being present through it all. Help me to experience your presence, even at the tomb. Amen.

Easter Vigil Darkness

Read John 20:1–11 and Luke 24:1–9.

They found the stone rolled away from the tomb, but when they went in, they did not find the body. (Luke 24: 2–3)

The Easter vigil is held sometime between sunset on Saturday and sunrise on Sunday, "while it was still dark." When the women are on the way to the tomb, they wonder who is going to roll the stone away from the tomb. It's a legitimate and understandable question. The stone is so heavy the two of them together won't be able to move it. I wonder if they are counting on a merciful Roman soldier to help them, or if their plan is to grab a passerby to help with the gruesome task before them: to go to the tomb to finish the burial preparation of their LORD and Savior.

When they get there, they find that the stone has already been rolled away. Instead of being glad, however, they are terrified. It's certainly not what they expected. Even though Jesus said it would happen that way, they fully assumed they would find a corpse in a sealed tomb. Now, in retrospect, more than two thousand years later, we all know exactly what happened! The miracle of our faith is that the tomb was and is empty, and this is indeed very good news! While it is still dark, though, our spirits would do well to walk with the women as they wonder who will roll the stone away. We cannot completely understand the joy of the empty tomb until we also comprehend the sad, despairing certainty the women must have felt as they approached Jesus' grave site. .

God of miracles, thank you for the empty tomb! Help me to dwell fully with the weight of the grave that I might understand it better. Amen.

Mystery

Read 1 Corinthians 15:51–54.

Listen, I will tell you a mystery! (v. 51a)

When I talk to parents struggling to communicate the basics of faith to their children, I encourage them to learn to embrace a single word—*mystery.* So much about our faith is completely unknowable to human beings. How did God create the world out of nothing? *Mystery.* How can Jesus be fully God and fully divine at the same time? *Mystery.* How was Jesus raised from the dead? *Mystery.*

Perhaps the most personal and profound mystery of all is this: What happens to us after we die? Paul explains it by saying we will not all die, but we will all be changed. This is the mystery.

On Easter morning all around the country, sermons are preached about new life, resurrection, and life after death. These sermons are inspiring and uplifting; they bring light to our darkness and hope to our despair, but for many, they are unsatisfying. I know this fact well even though I faithfully preach such a sermon every Easter. The reason these inspirational sermons are unsatisfying is that nobody—not me, not your pastor, not the Pope—nobody knows what happens after we die. Instead of trying to explain it, let's embrace the mystery of it and give thanks to God.

Lent is a journey, and so is this life. May we never forget that among the many gifts God has given us, we have been given one more—the gift of not knowing. There is freedom in the mystery.

Enjoy the journey.

In the name of the Father and of the Son and of the Holy Spirit, the Creator, Redeemer and Sustainer of us all. Amen.

Baptism and Confirmation Resources

Passage into Discipleship
Guide to Baptism
by Christopher W. Wilson

Passage into Discipleship helps older children and youth more faithfully prepare for the act of baptism by teaching what it means to walk a Christian journey. This book incorporates four different learning models that excite young people about becoming followers of Jesus.
Print ISBN 9780827230088, $14.99

Tour of Life
A Baptism and Confirmation Journey
by Jeff Wright

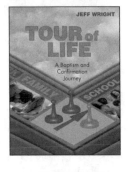

Tour of Life is an interactive learning experience for youth preparing for baptism or confirmation. It takes youth and their mentors on a journey through the seasons of life, with visits to a hospital nursery, a food ministry, a funeral home, and more to witness God's hand at work in all stages of life. *Tour of Life* draws youth and mentors alike into a deeper faith.
Print ISBN 9780827236615, $10.99

A Travel Guide to Christian Faith
by Dawn Weaks

A Travel Guide to Christian Faith has three components. The *Before You Go* booklet gives first-time seekers an easy-to-understand synopsis of the Christian faith. If they wish to learn more, the *Traveler's Edition* serves as a student workbook, while the *Tour Leader* is used by the instructor.

> "The guide takes travelers from the basic practices of faith, such as how to pray, all the way through baptism, discovering and applying spiritual gifts, and how to create your own 'rule' of spiritual life and holy habits. This set is a must for those churches and church leaders who are serious about helping the barely churched to connect with God, let alone to reaching the growing population of the never-churched."—Net Results

Before You Go 9780827217218, $3.99
Traveler's Edition 9780827217201, $11.99
Tour Leader 9780827217195, $11.99

CHALICE PRESS

1-800-366-3383 • www.ChalicePress.com
Ebooks also available

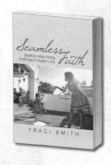

EVOCATIVE VOICES

The Young Clergy Women Project (TYCWP) Series

Who's Got Time?
Spirituality for a Busy Generation
by Teri Peterson and Amy Fetterman
Where does a relationship with God fit into our 24/7/365 living? *Who's Got Time?* offers new ways to incorporate spiritual practices into the busy lives of generations X, Y, and beyond.
Print ISBN 9780827243057, $16.99

Bless Her Heart
Life as a Young Clergy Woman
by Stacy Smith & Ashley-Anne Masters
Comprising essays from young women clergy, this book is a reflection on the everyday realities of pastoral ministry for the young, female professional.
Print ISBN 9780827202764, $15.99

Any Day a Beautiful Change
A Story of Faith and Family
by Katherine Willis Pershey
In this collection of personal essays, Katherine Willis Pershey chronicles the story of her life as a young pastor, mother, and wife. *Any Day a Beautiful Change* will strike a chord with anyone who has ever rocked a newborn, loved an alcoholic, prayed for the redemption of a troubled relationship, or groped in the dark for the living God.
Print ISBN 9780827200296, $14.99
www.katherinewillispershey.com

Making Paper Cranes
Toward an Asian American Feminist Theology
by Mihee Kim-Kort
This theological book engages the social histories, literary texts, and narratives of Asian American women, as well as the theological projects of prominent Asian American feminist theologians.
Print ISBN 9780827223752, $16.99   **www.miheekimkort.com**

CHALICE PRESS

1-800-366-3383 • www.ChalicePress.com
Ebooks also available